HOOD COUNTY PUBLIC LIBRARY

AF579987

S U N · S I G N

♍ ♍ ♍ ♍ ♍

SUN · SIGN

VIRGO

by james a. lely

creative education

♍ ♍ ♍ ♍ ♍

S U N · S I G N

Published by Creative Education, Inc., 123 South Broad Street, Mankato, Minnesota 56001 Printed in the United States.

Library of Congress Cataloging in Publication Data

Lely, James A
Virgo.

(Sun sign series)
SUMMARY: Describes the character and personality traits typical of the zodiacal sign Virgo.
1. Virgo (Astrology)—Juvenile literature.
[1. Virgo (Astrology) 2. Astrology] I. Title. II. Series.
BF1727.4.L44 133.5'2 77-12425
ISBN 0-87191-646-0

♍ ♍ ♍ ♍ ♍

S U N · S I G N

VIRGO

contents

♍ ♍ ♍ ♍ ♍

your sun sign is virgo

If your birthday is between
August 24 and September 23,
your sun sign is Virgo.
Your key word is "I analyze."
Your planet is Mercury.
Your element is earth.
Your symbol is the Virgin.
Your energy is mutable.
Your colors are greens, blue, beige, and white.
Your metal is platinum.
Your flower is the hyacinth.
Your stone is jade.

You are the restful oasis in the zodiac.
You are the one who will delight members
of all other signs
with your decency, stability, calmness, and innocence.

You have been referred to as the "hot water bottle"
of the zodiac because your restful manner
brings peace to members of the flightier signs.
Yet a close observer studying your face
might catch fleeting expressions
which betray secret worries.
You are not quick to form close, permanent
relationships, but you are devoted for life
once you decide to take the plunge.
You are especially fond
of the people in your family
and can sometimes be accused of smothering them.
You have gentle and attractive ways.
Rarely do you talk too much.
You are never disturbingly loud or raucous.
You are uncomfortable in crowds and sometimes
you even slip silently away when you need breathing space.

You appear to be simple and manageable,
yet you are elusive.
You look wiry, and have startlingly clear,
quiet eyes.
You are concerned about your physical
well-being
and make an effort to stay in good health.
You are generally well coordinated.
You have no lack of grace and charm;
you invented quiet good manners.
While you have a natural humility,
you are sometimes caught by vanity.
You are always dressed well, but
conservatively;
you prefer subdued colors which are found in
nature.
You look best with stark white against your
face.
You may even be fussy
about the clothes you choose to be sloppy in.

You are not a large person, but you have
much
more physical and character strength
than is apparent from your slight frame.

Your stamina is astounding
especially in your work.
Your work is the center of your life.

You must find outlets for your worries—
since you don't talk easily to people
(except those closest to you).
You tend to choose interests which will
keep you active.
Simple deep breathing
may relieve many of the nameless anxieties
you sometimes feel.

Although you are dependable and sincere,
you are
known to pretend to be falling asleep,
or suffering from a dreadful headache,
when you are doing something you don't like
to do—
such as being with a lot of people.
Surprisingly, however, when you leave that
boring party,
you get every bit of your energy back,
and the headache always disappears!

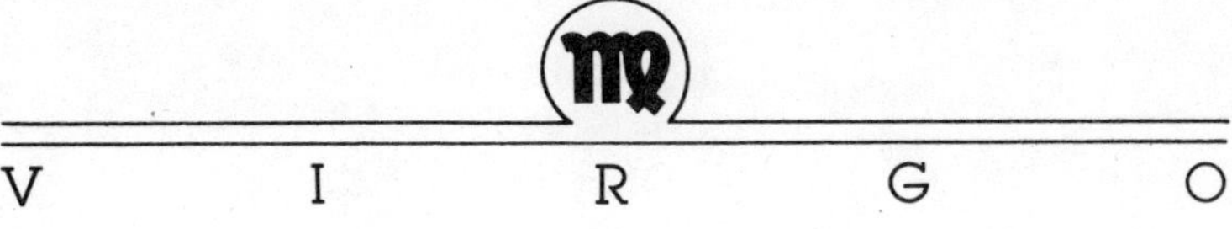

You have the clever Mercury wit,
and if you like the people with you,
you will entertain them hilariously.
This wit, though, is sometimes used sarcastically
especially on people whose behavior
does not meet with your approval.

You are scandalized by extravagance,
either in behavior or with money.
When going on a trip, you will always drive,
take a bus or train rather than fly.
You are obsessed with conservative use of cash
and are prudent to an extreme.
You expect good service from others
because you are so service-minded yourself.

You judge people sternly, but you like
a wide range of people.
You don't bear grudges and,
when the facts are in, you are fair.

In an argument, a Virgo can be painfully hairsplitting,
but if you detect that your
opponent is being damaged by your argument,
you will instantly come around
and make him or her comfortable again.
It's instinctual for you to want to serve other's needs.

You may develop peculiar inhibitions,
because a Virgo isn't well-suited
to all the Mercury influences.
You aren't really comfortable with your dreams
of free, foot-loose living,
and this causes some inner anxieties.
Many astrologers feel that Virgo is really ruled
by Vulcan, the Planet of thunder.
When that planet is discovered, they say,
Virgos will be relieved
of much of their present nervous tensions.
Vulcan may also give Virgos
a broader scope for their qualities
of courage and confidence.

It is interesting that Vulcan is a lame-footed god
and that many Virgos have either a limp
or some unusual way of walking.

Although your loyalty knows no comparison,
you give love quietly and steadily,
with little demonstrativeness.
Many of your sign choose to remain unmarried.
If you do marry,
you will be a dominant influence in your home
because you need to feel needed.
you are glad to give services,
but because you are unsure of yourself,
you usually resent receiving them.
You are the same with gifts,
especially on your birthday.
You imagine that there are strings attached
to everything someone does for you.
You want to be independent,
yet your very nature
drives you to seek security
and to desire affection by someone you love and do not fear.

You are self-critical, and that criticism
is usually totally out of proportion
to your actual problems.
You are basically simple and well ordered
yet clutter your life with many unnecessary
details.

You like cats and other helpless small
animals.
You like truth, punctuality, economy,
prudence, and discretion.
You hate gushy sentiment,
dirt, vulgarity, and idleness.
You are the one to straighten the picture or
wipe off a speck of dust when visiting
someone's home.
The only time you are sloppy is when you are
unhappy.
Once you've learned to master life's
complicated details
instead of letting details master you,
you can shape your destiny with more
certainty
than any other sign.

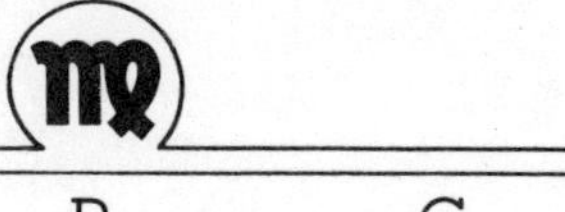

Although you hate moving, you tend to move great distances when the atmosphere gets too close for you.
You aren't willing to try other means to clear the air.

Cool green jade and pure platinum complement you
and bring you luck.
You are as clear as glass to some types of people,
but you prefer to think that you are secretive.
Those who have been close to you never forget you,
and you, in turn, remain faithful to them.
You have a way of making people remember you;
few will forget your fragrance.

but you're probably not 100% virgo

Do you recognize yourself? If you were born between August 24 and September 23, you may share most of the personality traits typical of Virgo. But you probably feel that you don't share all of them. This is not too surprising.

Knowing that someone is a Virgo or a Taurus is similar to knowing that he is Japanese, Italian, or Egyptian. A person's nationality tells you something about what the person might look like and how he might think and act. Someone who is Irish might have black hair, a round face and freckles. Someone who is of Scottish descent might be thrifty.

Yet knowing a person's nationality won't tell you everything. Not all people of the same nationality share the same traits. To get a clearer picture of the person, you would have to find out about the person's age, sex, religion, favorite sport and hobbies.

In the same way, a person's sun sign

can provide some general information. But it cannot reveal all of the aspects of a personality. If an astrologer wanted to know more about a person, he or she would have to find out exactly when and where the person was born. Then the astrologer would calculate the exact position of the sun, the moon and the planets of our solar system in relation to the earth at the moment of the person's birth.

Astrologers believe that human beings are affected by the same energies that cause the sun, the moon and the planets to move in their orbits. They believe that a chart showing the position of these heavenly bodies at the moment of birth can be a kind of blueprint giving clues to a person's personality and potential.

But drawing up such a chart is no easy matter, since the earth, as well as the sun, moon and planets, are all constantly in motion. Because of this movement, even identical twins born only minutes apart will have slightly different birth charts, and two Virgos whose birthdays are ten days apart can be very different indeed.

Interpreting a birth chart is even more complicated than constructing it. That's why many astrologers advise beginners to start their study of astrology by learning about sun signs. Since the sun affects life on the earth more than the other stars and the planets do, the sun sign is a very important factor in a birth chart. Just remember that it's not the only factor.

One more word of caution: it takes approximately 29 days for the sun to move through each of the twelve zones or sun signs of the zodiac. But the exact time when the sun passes from one zone to the next varies from year to year, so the dates listed for any sun sign are only approximate.

If you were born on August 24, you might be either Virgo or Leo, and if your birthday is September 23, your sun sign could be Virgo or Libra. In order to tell for sure which you are, you would have to consult an astrological reference book called an ephemeris. After making certain corrections depending on precisely where you were born, you would have to look up your exact time of birth in order to see whether the sun had changed signs by then.

If you were born at one of these turning points and don't have access to an ephemeris, try reading about both signs. See if you can tell which description fits you better.

Your sun sign can't tell you everything about yourself. But it can give some general characteristics. In reading about your sun sign you may come to know and understand yourself better.

what you may look like

Your sun sign affects your physical appearance, as well as your personality. Just remember that there are other factors at work and that you probably won't look exactly like this typical Virgo portrait.

The typical Virgo has:

— a long face with well-defined jawline
— unusually clear and bright eyes
— a short, turned-up nose
— delicate and sensitive lips and high cheekbones
— strong hands and long, squared fingers
— a healthy, athletic and trim figure, carefully maintained
— a winning and gentle smile
— an expression that suggests that a slightly troublesome secret is closeted inside
— stern eyebrows

what you might expect

Your sun sign also affects the way you think and act. As you read the following descriptions of how a Virgo might act in certain situations, see if you can recognize yourself. But remember this is a hypothetical person. Don't look for a mirror image of yourself. You will probably only catch glimpses of the you you know.

school

With dread you await the final tests for the semester or quarter. You always take detailed notes and review them frequently. On the day-to-day quizzes your scores will always be high. You understand each little point, but have trouble seeing how things tie together—what the "larger picture" is.

Your conscientiousness is every teacher's delight: you come on time to class, you are well behaved, you are cooperative. You are weak in subjects requiring a great deal of imagination. If you are bored with a class, however, you make earnest efforts to get yourself into the mood. Your handwriting may be a thing of beauty, and your typed assignments are flawless. Surprisingly, though, you may have trouble spelling due to the little amount of attention you pay to the extra reading which builds vocabulary.

Because you have such a strong devotion to duty, you are often selected to take charge of a class in a teacher's absence. You will also be called on to tutor students because you are patient with someone who is trying to learn.

Just because you are absent from a class doesn't mean that you're skipping out on school work. You have probably been excused to participate in a student council meeting. Or you might be thoroughly checking the final edition of the school newspaper, of which you are probably the editor. You are interested in school government, and you may even come out of your shy shell to run for an office. You are involved in many school activities, always present at the homecoming game and to clean up after a dance.

Your good study habits will secure you honors and perhaps later scholarships to colleges. When you pick your college, it will be either a private one or a smaller college in a university. Although dormitory life will appeal to your desire to be near the center of things, the loss of privacy will soon persuade you to hand over the money for more expensive housing where you can be alone.

You like school and will work hard to achieve good grades. You may even want to stay in school for an unusual length of time. While you may detect that out beyond school even a sheltered Virgo may find challenges, you will still hesitate to change your status as you intuitively know that there is no going back.

travel

You'll never invite a crowd to the airport or dock to see you off on a journey, because your reason for taking the trip is to give yourself a chance to be alone and reflective. Your favorite part of a trip is the time spent getting there. You feel as if time has been suspended and that all pressures have been lifted. If you are travelling with a companion, this is the time when you will be the most withdrawn and untalkative.

Even though you are comfortable and active in school, you may notice a timid streak just before going on a class trip. Your sense of security may be shaken and you may be stricken with homesickness the first several times away. When you arrive at your destination, you don't care to have your schedule filled with group tours or planned sightseeing. Either alone or with a friend, you will drift off and see a few sights on you own.

A Virgo won't buy a teddy bear with "Greetings from Atlantic City" written in glitter on its stomach. Souvenirs don't appeal to you for you have no need of visible reminders of a trip once you return home. However, you will spend a budgeted amount of money on gifts for friends, and maybe a small treat for yourself. After all, if travelling is your means of getting back in touch with yourself, what is more appropriate than a little self indulgence?

After a trip, the Virginian tendency is to return home as fast as possible. There you will find all familiar, comforting things. This is why you are so reluctant to move. Remember the Virgo trait of stability—and nothing is more nerve-wracking and shaking than to pack up and move.

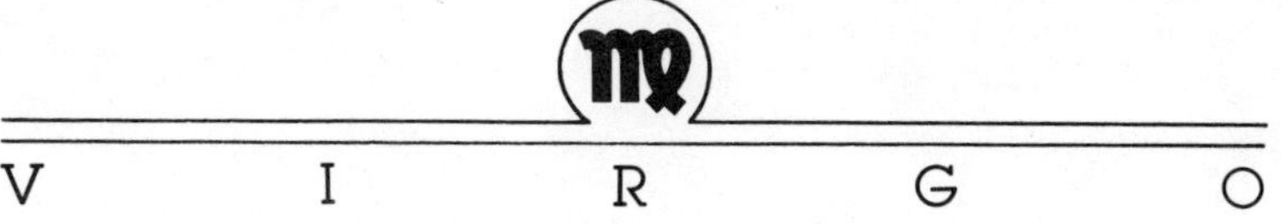
V I R G O

likes and dislikes

It can never be said that a Virgo is a non-stop compulsive spender. If you are out shopping and spot something you've been considering purchasing, you won't hesitate to buy it, but you will be happy that you didn't behave extravagantly. You never spend money just because it is in your pocket. Your generosity is a becoming virtue when it comes time to give gifts. You would never spend as much on yourself as you will on someone else, and you take real joy in using this method of pleasing people.

You rebel, however, at the traditional gift-giving times, and may spend only a quarter as much on someone's Christmas or birthday gift as you will on an "It's Good to Know You" present given at no special time.

You aren't too particular about what you listen to, but tend to choose records for the effect they give—background music for working, melancholy singing, carefree instrumental works.

You appreciate fine things to be worn and touched, and your wardrobe is always subdued and in excellent taste. You feel good in well-made clothing designed for the current season. Even though your clothes should last longer than that season, you derive security and comfort from knowing that your new outfit complements your natural beauty. You will spend money on jewelry, but it is the type that needs a second glance to fully appreciate its worth—never flashy.

Your delicate digestive systems steers you away from rich and spicy foods, but you are always willing to try new recipes for milder foods which you consider "safe." Your attention to detail gives you the ability to appreciate well-prepared foods, from souffle to caramels.

You are not eager to engage in new activities which mean exposure to many people and will never participate in party games. But there are many activities you enjoy from skydiving to reading fiction.

sports and hobbies

You prefer sports which give you an opportunity to work off your tensions alone. Besides swimming, tennis and handball, you will enjoy such vigorous activities as gymnastics, acrobatics, climbing, and even ping pong. In the winter your chief delights will be skating and skiing; in the summer you hike through at least one pair of boots.

You will struggle to master dance of all kinds: ballet, contemporary ballet, ballroom, and tap. You are never satisfied until you can perform something flawlessly, and will practice tirelessly.

Your quieter activities are again related to your earth sign. Birdwatching is a natural for you, as is watercolor painting. You may distract yourself by writing poetry or reading philosophy, always wondering what the practical applications are. Another hobby

will likely be learning to play a musical instrument. You don't devote your life to it but will struggle and take lessons with your usual fine discipline.

A hobby which requires cataloging and picky sorting probably wouldn't put you off. But you might be more interested in collecting things for the purpose of learning about other places or staying in contact with friends who live or are visiting out of town. One good example is postcard collecting; once people know that you are interested, you'll be hearing from a variety of places.

Your rich earth sign will give you a tendency to grow plants. After you buy your plants and bring them home, they are subjected to much tender loving care. You polish the leaves, pick off dead blossoms, and may give them as much attention as you would give a child. Naturally, they thrive on that treatment. Your friends will be frequently pleased with this particular hobby of yours, as you are known to give cuttings replanted in lovely pots.

virgo friendships

Because of your natural shyness and your uncompromising standards for others, you are normally a person of few friends. You will keep a sharp eye on people getting close to you and will probably not unfold your full personality for a long time—until you are sure that you are entirely safe. However, when you do decide to give in to the call of friendship, you begin to enjoy yourself completely.

You are attracted to people who not only see what is hidden behind your seemingly peaceful expression, but who are also gifted and certainly more outgoing than you. Sometimes you are a follower rather than a leader and need to have strong people as your friends. You have emotional needs but tend not to express them. Sometimes you are critical of others' emotional expressions. Since you take care of yourself, you often expect others to take care of themselves, too.

In your relationships with others, you are more responsive to a touch or other quiet communication than to a rousing conversation. You can talk about the details of your work, but have trouble expressing yourself on more serious topics. You have fine intuitions but may not trust them. Some astrologers say that this is the result of Mercury's influence—it leads you away from trusting your hunches.

You have great passion of the spirit, and you deeply care for your friends but will rarely openly demonstrate your affection. Once you've allowed someone to get close to you, you expect him or her to be secure and not to need constant reassurance of your loyalty. You are mysterious and quiet and are usually lonely even in the company of two or three close friends.

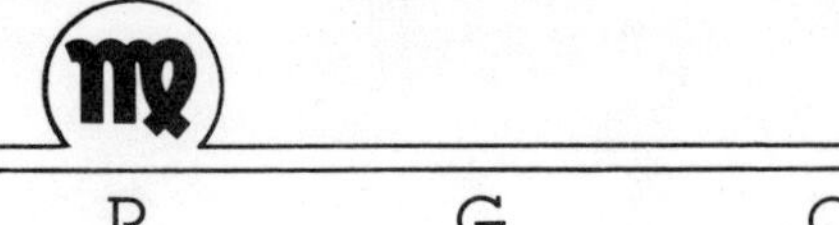

A Virginian is highly trustworthy and will always be found as the intimate of people in responsible, complex positions. You will be critical of your friends. However, you do not take negative criticism well, as your insecurities are too easily stirred. People who correct you must be very careful in choosing their words if they do not wish to hurt your feelings.

You are known as a heartbreaker: people eager to get near you must prove themselves. Yet when you have spotted a prospective friend and have completed your watching and testing, you call upon all of your hidden charm and insist on winning him or her as soon as possible.

You won't tolerate nagging, and if a friendship starts to break up, you will run from any unpleasantness. Sometimes it seems that you'll do anything to avoid discomfort.

Here's what you like to do with friends:

— have long, thoughtful talks in front of a fireplace
— visit a zoo or go on a picnic
— play tennis or handball
— go swimming
— hear a concert or see a play

Here's what you don't like to do:

— go to a noisy party
— meet new people
— eat at crowded restaurants
— play baseball
— go on wild shopping sprees

In short, you are a good "best friend" type although you are reluctant to be tolerant of the differences in others. As you become more secure you will become more understanding, but you will always have to work at tolerance.

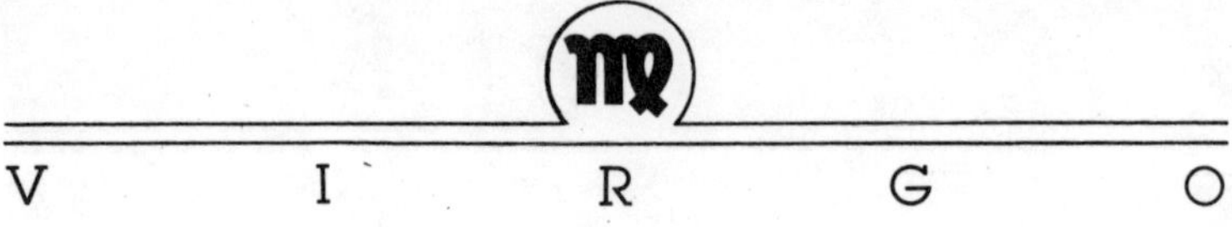

health - Rx for virgo

Because you cannot verbally express the things which trouble you, it is vital that you find some other outlet for your tension. As you don't care especially for team sports, other vigorous choices such as handball, tennis, or swimming are appropriate. You will play until you are exhausted and then return home with renewed energy to tolerate any problems. You always think clearer after taking care of your body.

Your emotional condition has a direct relationship to your digestive tract, which is normally very sensitive. You probably have an aversion to fatty meats and artificial food. You prefer fish, lean meats, and plenty of fruits and vegetables. If you get a cold, it is very important to take good care of yourself for you usually respond poorly to large doses of medication. Lungs are a weak point for you. You are especially susceptible to ailments of the hips, arms, shoulders, and back, and probably bang yourself up quite a bit. You may be a likely candidate for arthritis unless you stay fit and limber.

Despite the extraordinary attention which a Virgo will pay to it, your health is the best in the zodiac. You may have been a sickly child, but you will get stronger and remain well for the rest of your life.

♍

V I R G O

other virgos like you

Some of your Virgo tendencies will be more noticeable when you're young. Others will become apparent as you grow older. Some traits will be especially evident in certain roles or occupations. See if you can identify typical characteristics in other Virgos you may know.

if your father is a virgo

You probably have two cars in your garage. To satisfy his sense of responsibility, he bought a sensible, practical economical car. The other car, however, may be harder for him to explain. His passion may run to a flashy sports car, which will satisfy the mercurial influences. He works steadily at his job and is well liked and respected. You find him stern and distant, and probably notice that although he gives your more expressive mother the main responsibility of raising you, his love is genuine and deep. Don't expect him to be openly affectionate, however.

Although you can expect irritation when you bring home a busload of friends, you know you can count on his help with your mathematics and science homework. And you can be sure he will always stand by you in times of trouble.

if your younger brother is a virgo

You'll have to learn to live with his uncertain health. He will have a cold half the time, and a banged-up knee or hand the other half. Virgos are always getting scrapes on the knuckles and other joints. He'll get into at least his fair share of mischief, but won't be found running around in a gang of others his age. He enjoys painting by himself on those lazy afternoons. He is visually oriented and will never hear when you call him. He will always be the first to know when you're up to something you shouldn't be, and his natural indignation will send him running to tell on you. If he sees you're really in a jam, though, he'll try to help you out of it, as he is designed to be of service to others.

if your teacher is a virgo

You'd better hope that you are on time for class! There'll be little nonsense in your room. She respects talent and those who try hard, but has a short temper with laziness. You'll find her very likeable, despite the fact that you got her hardest glare for whispering behind her back. She's not one to embarrass a student with public humiliation, but a sarcastic word might land your way now and then. Don't take it too hard, as she is fond of her pupils and stays up nights wondering if she's doing her job properly. It may be old-fashioned, but give her an apple—noisy students tend to give her a headache!

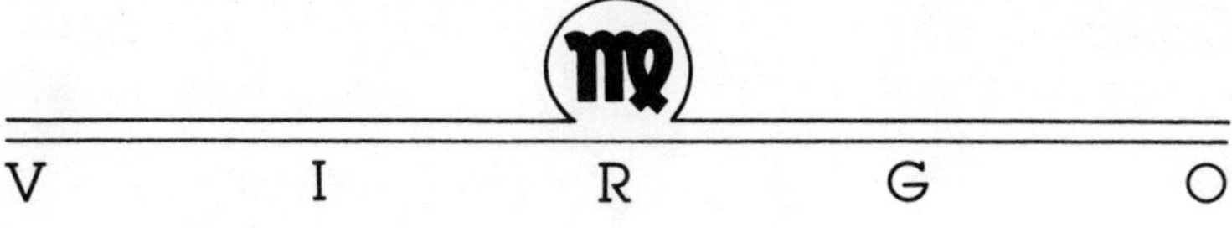

virgo careers

You spend a lot of time fretting over whether or not to take the job, because you are uncomfortable with having to pull up roots and start looking again. You are not likely to ask yourself if you've made a mistake once you've started working.

A Virgo is recognized as the most loyal, most devoted to duty, and most capable "man-behind-the-scenes" employee any company could hire. Because of your reluctance to be exposed to the public, you may not choose a job with selling in it. You are basically humble and expect to start at the bottom and work up. An employer who spots you as having great potential is making a mistake by showering you with promotions, bonuses, and other privileges. You will become suspicious of such an employer and feel that you are unprepared for the tasks at hand. You may have the feeling of walking on very thin ice despite the obvious respect and confidence your boss has in you. You prefer to prove to yourself that you are capable of making a success out of your job.

You are both analytical, with great attention to details, and eager to be of service. You are a likely Chairman of the Board, directing the shape of the policy makers' decisions, but an unlikely President, as you hate the direct line of fire and the intense exposure. You are often found in the Accounting Department of a company. Well-equipped with prudence and temperance, you hold in the reins on your more impulsive superiors. You can be trusted with anything, and have ideals too high to ever let anyone down.

Here are some other careers where you may find yourself:

- — publishing
- — the literary field
- — medicine—research, doctor, nurse, technician
- — pharmacy
- — any of the food preparations or science areas
- — laboratory work—pure science research
- — bookkeeping and accounting
- — social work on a one-to-one basis
- — travel agent—although you may be surprised at how luxuriously others live
- — commercial and detailed private artistry
- — any maintenance work, with the more need for detail the better
- — most service agencies requiring a sympathetic but practical eye

famous people born under the sign of virgo

Prince Albert, husband of Queen Victoria
Alexander the Great, explorer
Robert Benchley, humorist
Ingrid Bergman, actress
Leonard Bernstein, conductor
Terry Bradshaw, football player
Maurice Chevalier, actor
Theodore Dreiser, author
Queen Elizabeth I of England

Henry Ford II, wealthy businessman
Greta Garbo, actress
Arthur Godfrey, comedian
Goethe, author
Lyndon B. Johnson, 36th President of U.S.
Joseph Kennedy, ambassador
Lafayette, explorer
D.H. Lawrence, author
Sophia Loren, actress
H.L. Mencken, author
Bob Newhart, comedian
Peter Sellers, comedian
Robert Taft, politician
William Howard Taft, 27th President of U.S.
Tolstoi, author
Roy Wilkins, civil rights leader

sun signs for young people

creative education

ARIES • March 21 — April 20
TAURUS • April 20 — May 21
GEMINI • May 21 — June 21
CANCER • June 21 — July 23
LEO • July 23 — August 23
VIRGO • August 24 — September 23
LIBRA • September 23 — October 23
SCORPIO • October 23 — November 22
SAGITTARIUS • November 22 — December 22
CAPRICORN • December 22 — January 20
AQUARIUS • January 20 — February 18
PISCES • February 18 — March 20